PERFECT, BROKEN OR IN JAGGED FRAGMENTS

poems by

Elizabeth P. Buttimer

Finishing Line Press
Georgetown, Kentucky

PERFECT, BROKEN OR IN JAGGED FRAGMENTS

Copyright © 2019 by Elizabeth P. Buttimer
ISBN 978-1-63534-984-9 First Edition
All rights reserved under International and Pan-American Copyright Conventions. No part of this book may be reproduced in any manner whatsoever without written permission from the publisher, except in the case of brief quotations embodied in critical articles and reviews.

ACKNOWLEDGMENTS

To the following publications and journals in which some of the poems in this chapbook have first, appeared appreciation and grateful acknowledgment is made.

Magnolia Quarterly: "How Many Boxes Does It Take;" "Whiskey Street and Hog Liver Road;" "The Man Who Wears Bow Ties;" "The Merchant Muses on Women Writing"
Haunted Waters Press: "Ars Poetica, How to Wear a Scarf"
Splash: "Despite His Good Ole Boy Ways, You Just Can't Trust Him"
Blue Mountain Review: "The Far Crossing"
Raw Art Review: "The Far Crossing"

I want to express my gratitude to the many generous friends that I have made in the poetry community who have helped inspire and inform my writing. I want to thank the Atlanta Writer's Club, the Georgia Poetry Society and the Palm Beach Poetry Festival . I am especially appreciative to G.M., N.B., K.H., C.W., P.M.K., Betsy Bairstow Morse, Donna Reed, Meg Skinner and Vicki Young and all those who have encouraged, taught and mentored me.

Deo gratias.

Publisher: Leah Maines
Editor: Christen Kincaid
Cover Art: Elizabeth P. Buttimer
Author Photo: Linda Carroll, LC Photography
Cover Design: Tiggio Design—Antonio Marshall

Printed in the USA on acid-free paper.
Order online: www.finishinglinepress.com
also available on amazon.com

Author inquiries and mail orders:
Finishing Line Press
P. O. Box 1626
Georgetown, Kentucky 40324
U. S. A.

Table of Contents

To the Craftsman 1

Praise for the New Day 2

The Man in the Moon 3

Bower of Roses 4

She Wears His Name like a Golden Crown 6

How Many Boxes Does It Take 7

The Young Beauty Sees Her Future 8

Ars Poetica, How to Wear a Scarf 9

The Depths 10

Whiskey Street and Hog Liver Road 11

Despite His Good Ole Boy Ways, You Just Can't Trust Him 12

The Man in the Red Sailboat 13

Reckless 14

The Man Who Wears Bow Ties 15

The Merchant Muses on Women Writing 16

The Creative Urge 17

Unexpected Forecast 19

Soft Moonlight from the Window 20

The Place Where No Trees Grow 21

Viewing From the Promontory 22

While She Remembers Sweetness 23

Returning Empty Vessels 24

The Far Crossing 25

Illumination 27

This is a work of fiction. Names, characters, places, events, locales, and incidents are either the products of the author's imagination or used in a fictitious manner. Any resemblance to actual persons, living or dead, or actual events is purely coincidental.

*With love to Dan, Christopher, my late parents, my family, friends, teachers, and all who supported my efforts in writing and taught me to sing a melodious sonnet.
May the road rise to meet you.*

To the Craftsman

From these bricks that lie in front of me
the timbers resting a few feet away
the nearby wet-mud grainy, thick and creamy
With my level, tools, and dusty plans
I will raise up a new home
with nails that pierce and put
windows and doors that open and shut
saws that sever and shape
and tin for the roof
I will raise up a new home
a sanctuary for my breath and body
with rough, craggy hands,
sun kissed raisin skin and with
the help of friends working together
a foundation, four walls, a roof and a floor
create my masterpiece and the raindrops
resounding on the tin, my opus.

Praise for the New Day

At the edge of "Peace and Plenty" farm,
an abandoned brick house sits in disarray.
The thatched roof fell in bit by bit
and nature began its reign again.
Warm sunshine, soft rain and heavy
storm weathered the old home.
Brick by brick, the structure began
to give way; as the mortar wearied
of holding hands.

Some say the place is in decay
but I am resolved that it is in
transformation. The walls and pillars
remaining, look like remnants
of an ancient castle, the hallmark
of forgotten craftsmen.

A small rabbit finds habitation
in what was once the front hall.
Errant ferns and flowers have
sprouted unexpectedly.
Birds nest atop the pinnacle's edge,
praising the new day by
singing their morning matins,
while the worn walls
give refuge to the angels,
who rest lightly there
as they survey the daffodils.

The house loosens it's heavy load,
brick by brick, board by board,
This aged shell mellowed
into an open air abode for angels,
a sanctuary for wings.

The Man and the Moon

I see stars
when I look in your eyes
that twinkle
as I walk with green cheese
under my feet,
covering my boots
with dazzling emerald dust,
more brilliant than
sequins,
brighter still,
the way I feel when
you're near.
I look down to earth
through midnight blue sky
knowing when you take
me by my hand, we are weightless,
no-tether to the
ground
we are star-flung
sky and
space.
Those mere earthlings,
    what do they know
        of the surface of the moon?
 Wearing their
   humdrum-grey
        pajamas,
basking in your lambent glow,
     they marvel at mysteries of the heavens.
        Tell me, how can those drab tellurians ever fathom our galaxy?

Bower of Roses

Let me build for you
a white board and batten cottage
with green shutters, and a red door
only a few blocks from the sea.
I will build the foundation
brick by brick with love.
With each nail I drive
into the wood, I will breathe
a prayer for your happiness
and for our children yet to be.
With each floor board
I will join your love and mine
dovetailing them together
plank by plank to make
your path instilled by tenderness
and your footsteps always cherished.

Each step will bring us
nearer to knowing and loving.
Building each stair,
will take me step by step closer
to the sky and stars
to write large my love
and high my praise for you.
In our bedroom facing toward the sea,
you find welcome rest beside me,
soothed by the rhythm
of waves. I will be reassured
by your quiet breathing.

Your breath and the sea breeze
gentle and restoring.
Your head nestled on my shoulder,
as your chest rises and falls
in rhythm with the sea and me.
I caress you in the haven of our hearts,
our home by the sea, the white bungalow
with a bower of roses by the front door,
sweet scented canopy of red sueded petals.

She Wears His Name like a Golden Crown

and her mantle, as his wife,
like the center jewel,
a pigeon's blood ruby
whose verve pounds stronger
than the hearts of two oxen,
well-yoked, pulling a load
of cornerstones in a wooden cart,
with gaily painted wheels of red,
white and yellow, caked in mud
from the mucky jungle path.

The oxen, as they step-in-tandem,
bob and sway their heads,
left-and-right, right-and-left,
each ringing small brass bells,
that adorn the joined pair,
with shared jingling for their journey.
Set among the golden tassels,
tiny brasses, nestled in red silk braids
of the oxen's bright coronas,
tintinnabulate their union's tempo.

How Many Boxes Does It Take

to hold a love letter a day for forty years?
Written in the same hand steady, or scrawled,
what do we know of love lived as a marathon
not as a sprint across one page? Written apurpose,
all those words on all those pages,

delivered across a room or in a restaurant,
over dirty dishes in the kitchen sink,
on a pillow, or a stack of clean diapers
on a sleepless night, tucked in a suitcase,
or in a Bible, packed in a briefcase
full of forecasts, projections and trends.

Overnight or overseas on a battlefield,
or a minefield of Mondays
strung in a row for years,
love letters mailed from cities and hamlets
across oceans and continents, rivers
and bridges between a man and a woman,
day in and day out, fair weather and foul.

A promise became a habit early on,
trying to find a boat over the gulf
of gender, walking on the water
to reach each other and wrap love
in an envelope sealed with a kiss.
How many boxes does it take
to hold a love letter a day for forty years?
How many boxes does it take to hold a lifetime?

The Young Beauty Sees Her Future

As she rubs the old rag
round and round the brass-work
wet with acrid polish,
stained black, by tarnish,
round and round the brass-work
on the heavy wooden door,
she yearns to find a man
with greater prospects
a man of property and substance
even an old man or a fragile old man
whose last days she could fulfill.

She lifts her dark eyes from the door.
She stands, smooths her starched
black uniform and white apron
shakes her long tresses,
pushes back her shoulders,
dips her neck like a swan,
smiles demurely, and beckons
with onyx eyes at the white haired
gentleman leaning ponderously
on his gold-handled, black-lacquered
cane and beyond him to the muscled
gardener pushing a laden red wheelbarrow.

Ars Poetica, How to Wear a Scarf
for JBB

John says scarves should be worn
with reckless abandon,
like whirling the constellations
over your shoulder in one swoosh,
like casting a net for crabs
or loosely folding whipped egg whites.

He says scarves should not be worn
like origami folds a tiny bird
nor breeders mate thoroughbreds,
nor as a bomb squad carries a package
nor a sniper aims, calculating wind speed
nor counted-cross-stitch inhabits muslin.

John says a scarf should be worn
with reckless abandon,
like you toss kisses to a child
or jettison a drained glass
into the fire shouting "*Opa!*"
or run to aid a stranger
collapsing in the street
or a piccolo trills in a Sousa March
like firefighters charge flames
casting fear on a pyre of mother-in-law-tongues
like you throw yourself into rising waters
or the way you rashly thrust into love again.

The Depths

At tempest,
the ocean churns
wildly first, then,
rhythmically,
over and over,
bottom to top,
strewing shells
and debris
on the shore,
like memories of you
which surface roughly
from the depths,
sometimes perfect,
broken, or in
jagged fragments.

Whiskey Street and Hog Liver Road

Mama told me what a man like you would be like,
who lived at the corner of Whiskey Street and Hog Liver Road.
Rough hands and rough ways, probably chews tobacco, she says
drinks corn liquor, swears and works on Sunday.
She said to beware of your wayward ways.
I dutifully said that I would but how could I know?
Your sweet talk was so smooth,
as smooth as your hands were rough.
Why did I find those rugged hands,
calloused with a sandpaper edge,
could rub off the hard edges of my resolve
and sand away my good sense?
Hands so rough, the edges so hard, rub so fine
not to leave a trace.

Despite His Good Ole Boy Ways You Just Can't Trust Him

Whatever you do, don't open the box.
That box could hold a bombshell
if you knew the man, like I do.
You would know it could be
anything, from rattlesnakes
to pixie-dust.

One thing for sure,
it isn't what he said it is.
It could be anything from chicken
feathers to ticking clocks
to battery acid or roller skates.
Maybe a pig's carcass,
albeit a small one, a baby
pig that died of natural causes
or maybe a leprechaun.

He could put a cuckoo clock
in there for all I know, fishing worms,
statues of Napoleon, or animal refuse,
really, you should be pleased
if it's just fertilizer, at least your garden
would welcome a heavy boxful.
Come harvest time,
you would see the benefit.

Boomerang or bowling ball,
cannon or Klondike bars,
pop goes the weasel or the weasel
himself. I would not open the box.
I would not even peep inside
or shake it to see if it rattles.
No, I would not open the box.
It isn't what he says it is.

The Man with the Red Sailboat

She screams loudly,

I killed him,
the man with the red sailboat.
I dashed his head upon the rocks
till blood flooded the crags
and red-red-life poured into the sea.
Red, the color of his sailboat, the one
that cut with the wind full in its sails
over azure sea skating high above
razor rocks, jagged shells, and detritus.

The red sailboat I used to share with him
before those razors, barbs and flotsam
huddled on the bottom of the sea
became all that was left, no calm waters.

Yes, I killed him the man with red sailboat.

I dashed his head upon the rocks
as he had done to us and pounded
his skull until his red-red-life poured
into the sea and his body lay still
for buzzards to pick at will, and seagulls
to roost beside. I killed him, she says,

but what she really means is I wish
I could kill him, I wish I could
wrap my hands around his throat
and squeeze until he breathes no more
or kisses me again like he once did.

Reckless

The fig bush greening its lush leaves in sun
spreads out its hand-shaped fronds to the air
full of expectant certitude of the day ripe fruit
will hang like kisses suspended in the breeze
by single stems caressing ovoid sweet meats.

Rain washes leaves and satisfies deep roots,
who hunger for moisture in the earth.
Days parade grandly or sometimes quietly pass
till verdant leaves turn to harvest time
when birds peck at fulsome fruits.

Until, a dark day some wild-eyed man
opens sharp-jawed pruning shears
hacking away as if the fig bush were kudzu
or unredeemed weeds or an errant poplar intruding
upon a rose garden. Who gave this crazy-man
sharp clippers, letting him loose among the green?

A foolish wild-eyed man who does not know
the shape of its leaf, wielding blade against bush.
A man who has never bitten its soft flesh
and tasted the fig's incomparable sweetness.

The Man Who Wears Bow Ties

could be mayor, knows everyone
and their families by name
especially the daughters, mostly
the pretty ones, watching them
closely, to remember their walk
or the way they hold their heads
just so, to look at him with
the same admiration they reserve
for a friend's father or favorite uncle.

he wallpapers his mind
with pictures of them, walking
or turning or looking up to him.
filling a void he can't name
that he used to fill with bourbon
and the look his young wife
gave him early on, till she filled
the hole in her life with vodka,
dead dreams and other men.
the man who wears bow ties,
could be mayor, he knows everyone
and their families by name.

The Merchant Muses on Women Writing

the man who sells guns internationally
says all writers are crazy or drunkards,
like his brother's wife, not like women
should be. he prefers his women wearing
blue or white and being musical, playing
flute, piano or harp, classically, works
of Berlioz or Vivaldi or Bach. no, writing
is not for ladies, or gentlemen either.
too much thinking, too much hiding inside,
lurking in the cupboards of the mind,
not knowing where the darkness may lead
or be stirred up and put on paper.
the man who deals in guns internationally
says all writers are crazy or drunkards.

The Creative Urge

Yes, he's dead, the sleazy papers say
CELEBRITY MURDERED
in bold headlines, same size they use
for alien invasions or royal weddings.
Reports are true, but not by my hand.
As if I would use a knife,
how could you accuse me?
Where's the air of mystery?
Why not something creative?
like murder by banana peel,
or mayhem by chocolate?
Why not suggest something
like the clever placement
of a hatpin in back of the skull
or an ink pen that shoots acid?
or a knitting-needle-jab
as ticket-to-the-netherworld
The use of a knife, far too plain,
even a dullard would use a poker,
buttonhook or letter opener.
Someone from afar could use
a catapult, drone or laser.
Plenty of people will be glad-to-see
he's gone, he rubbed them all wrong.
Anyone could have done
the dark deed, by telepathy,
if wishes were weapons.
No, it wasn't me, I didn't do it,
anyway never with a knife.
far too pedestrian,
for something more inventive
you'll have to look further afield.
Maybe, Colonel Mustard
in the library with a candlestick?

Or plot something more creative
like the heavy bloodstained statue
of a Tang Dynasty horse wielded
by a left-handed person with a limp,
wearing a clown costume or dressed as
Napoleon Bonaparte or Madame Curie.

Unexpected Forecast

The lights went out again
not quietly but with a loud bang
like a shotgun in close quarters
it happened a few days ago,
the same way, a loud blast,
almost in the same room
but then with only high winds
not like today's torrential rain,

water like earthbound pellets
shot from angels' b b guns
in rapid succession downward
through high winds.
When lights came on again,
we were saying *thank heavens*
but only for a moment, then, again,
the loud bang into blackness.
Still lashing, rain and wind
bend palm trees like rubber.

Then, lights once more blazed,
we went back to living
in grooved places, tread-worn,
wearing rain suits to stay as dry
as possible but that doesn't protect
against transformers blowing,
plunging us into darkness,
that doesn't defend us
from angry eyes, harsh din,
quick-stirring storms, out of nowhere,
violent blasts, booming tempests
occurring with no warning.

Soft Moonlight from the Window

She hung up the phone quickly, as he unlocked the door.
So drunk that night, he came home so very drunk
so late it was, past midnight, but she was ready,
stew bubbling on the stove and served him quickly.

He mumbling *my father never let me......my father
made me...*as he sucked stew from a spoon. Never-mind
she said until the bowl was done, all the while praying
for right words to say or things to do, *wouldn't a
hot bath be nice? so relaxing, let me draw the water
for you,* she bathed him like a baby, dipping the soft orange
rag into water lightly rubbing his back with warm cotton cloth.

He said, *when I got a job and moved into my
own place I bought a pound of bacon and fried it up.
I ate the whole platter's worth in one sitting. Dad couldn't
say a word. Yessiree, ate it, a whole pound by myself because he
rationed us to two pieces each. Never enough, never enough,*

Never-mind she said, *just smell the patchouli and lavender bath oil,
isn't that nice? Are you getting sleepy? I pulled back the covers
so you can rest.* Still praying for right words, praying
he would fall asleep quickly.

Squeezing her eyes shut, she did not want to see
the silver glint, that short barrel's metallic glimmer
illumined by soft moonlight streaming through the window
or glimpse his hand in bed on the butt of the pistol by
faint nightlight in the dressing room. Listening to every sound
with closed eyes, till rhythmic breathing was louder
than her pounding heartbeat. Next morning, at eight-thirty,
she telephoned a friend, collect, to say, *I'm okay, thanks,
it's alright, never-mind.*

The Place Where No Trees Grow

When divorce was a forbidden land
to which few people traveled
I was first, on both sides, in my family
to pack my suitcase, train case,
hatbox and birdcage then head off
to a lawyer's office and courthouse
down an untrodden path, ill-equipped,
mute to the unknown tongue
spoken in that murky wasteland
where no trees grew green or full
first to face the family as a new thing
a divorced woman, not a divorced lady,
          for that wasn't possible, then.

Never-mind, good reasons to travel there
six months after the big wedding, after
all the thank you notes were written.
Miss or Mrs. mattered then, on letters,
engraved stationary, society columns,
invitations and phone bills. Mother said,

*"young ladies go from the arms of their
parents, to the arms of their college dorm
mothers, to the arms of their husbands".*

They don't go down dark treeless roads
        to forbidden lands of divorce.
            They shouldn't,
            you shouldn't,
             all alone,
             go down.
             Go down
      no dark barren roads alone.
My parents decided to travel the road with me.

Viewing from the Promontory
For E.

Early that morning, at the quiet of dawn,
You survey the view from the deck to lake water, below
appearing through mist as lazy, glassy and burnt umber,
boat dock and lounge chairs,
ripples from floating leaves, dragon flies or trout.

        Hours later, a tornado, packs a direct hit.

                House timbers tear to matchsticks,

glass shards jettison to embed in grass,
                trees, flesh and walls.
Cars fly, roof shingles fling
                      like discarded playing cards
            Sheds sail airborne, photos,
      furniture, building blocks,
            to the wind and you,   taken
                  without farewell,

never to find you,
            never to find you
                      never to find you.

            in a whirlwind to Heaven,
              like Elijah,
                  where angels greet you.

While She Remembers Sweetness

She holds the sugar cube between her fingers
dipping it into black coffee by touching the edge
to dark liquid. Seeping, seeping till white sugar
turns tan then, disintegrates into mirrored
blackness. Ripples, ripples, to bottom,
Waves with circling spoon. She takes another cube,
repeats the process. Ripples, ripples to bottom.

She thinks of her brain and curses the hot coffee
changing the sugar to melted syrup. She thinks of her
family. How will they? Who can pick up the pieces?
Two cubes sweeten the coffee but nothing takes
the bitter taste away from her diagnosis.

Returning Empty Vessels

Food eases sorrow they say,
so does keeping busy
or time helps, as it ticks on,
melting like a biomorphic watch
sprung from Salvador Dali's hand.
Memories intrude as others speak
or music plays.

Words spin, those said and unsaid.
Comfort puts salve on raw nerves
lasting only as long as the casserole
brought by a neighbor.

Numbness, the best solace,
deadens the heart...for a while,
until pain re-enters, screeching of life.

The Far Crossing

Thankful to have sweet exile
on this side of the river, a moment
to linger on the red clay bank
gazing at the poplars and live oaks.
I stand alone, mostly, inhale honeysuckle
and tea olive, tasting clean air after rain
feasting my eyes on green leaves
and geese propelling the river
their ribbon wake follows, drawing me
closer to the water, closer to the fording.

I sometimes can make out the other side,
hear their laughter and singing, the light
from their fire. I hear Mother call me
as if I were in the yard by the mimosas.
My brother fishes from that distant shore.
He catches a mess of fish and shares tales
with Uncle Jake, the two of them draw a crowd
who lean in to see the size of the fish
and hear tales bigger than most could imagine
yet for the greater part they're all true.

Papa makes plans and meets with the elders
as they weigh the merits of new ideas.
I can just make out the seesaw of discussion.
I hear only a word or two but they nod their heads
so it all seems pleasant enough and productive.
They gather in a clearing maybe an amphitheater
nestled under big magnolias, the creamy flowers
scattered in polished leaves like prize eggs,
the heady aroma wafts over river and back to me.

Still, I tarry on my riverbank, smell the grande flora
on the breeze and hum a melodious sonnet
sung by flaming tongues. I linger in this sweet exile.

Away but not away, here and there, apart but not part fog caresses the river, hugging high up on the bank, almost touching my toes, lapping at the red clay. Nothing to see but brume, mist shrouds the far shore.

Illumination

There was no clock those last three months
no day or night, no sun or moon.
There was no tide with ebb and flow
only ebbing, always ebbing.
Slipping the veil ever lower
between the now and
the netherworld.
Only one bedroom,
curtains drawn,
with a single
window,
open to the
angels.

When the ebbing was nearly done, she said, "Can you see the lights around the bed?
They look like the aurora borealis."

Elizabeth P. Buttimer, an entrepreneur and former educator, received her Ph.D. from Georgia State University, her M.S.C. and B.A. from Auburn University. She received the 2018 Haunted Waters Press Poetry Open Award, winner of the 2018 Natasha Trethewey Award from the Atlanta Writer's Club and a 2019 finalist for the Natasha Trethewey Award, honorable mention in the 2018 William Faulkner Literary Award presented in New Albany Mississippi, first prize in poetry in the 2018 Cisco Writer's Contest, and first prize in the *Seven Hills Literary Review* contest for a children's picture book.

www.ingramcontent.com/pod-product-compliance
Lightning Source LLC
LaVergne TN
LVHW041513070426
835507LV00012B/1530